No Longer
A Victim

No Longer A Victim

by
Malcolm Smith

P. O. Box 471692
Tulsa, Oklahoma 74147-1692

No Longer A Victim
ISBN 1-880089-14-9
Copyright © 1992 by Malcolm Smith
Malcolm Smith Ministries
P. O. Box 29747
San Antonio, Texas 78229

Published by:
Pillar Books & Publishing Co.
P. O. Box 471692
Tulsa, Oklahoma 74147-1692
United States of America

Cover design: DB & Associates

Book production: sigma graphics, ltd.

Editor: Elizabeth Sherman

TABLE OF CONTENTS

Chapter Four

CONFRONTING GOD 29

Chapter Five

DIVINE COOPERATION 37

Chapter Six

JOINING WITH GOD 47

No Longer
A Victim

Chapter One

FREEDOM FROM SELF-PITY

Do you see yourself as having wasted your life? Is your life a series of rejections by those you wanted to love you? Have you been abused by those from whom you expected protection and comfort? Do you despise and wish revenge on those who abused you? Have you resented God, believing He allowed the pain and suffering because He didn't love you enough to save you from it?

Many of us have lived through years of hell on earth scarred by abuse and riddled with tragedy. Then, we have added compound interest to all of those tragedies by resenting God, by building up bitterness toward the people who have hurt us, and by settling into a life of self-pity. As if that were not enough, we have envied those whom we have perceived as having a better life than ours.

A Biblical Case of Self-Pity

In John 5:1-11, there is an interesting story of Jesus healing a man with such an outlook on life. The story takes place at the pool of Bethesda in Jerusalem, where tradition had it that an angel came into the pool at unannounced times. It was said that whenever the angel came, whoever should first step into the pool as the waters were being mysteriously disturbed would be healed.

The large patio around the pool was filled with the sick, along with their friends and relatives...all waiting for the moment of miracle. It was to this place that Jesus came on a certain day and made His way to a man who had been a cripple for thirty-eight years. The pool had become both his hope and his address.

Jesus asked this man an odd question: **Do you wish to get well?** (John 5:6). Another translation is, "Are you in earnest about getting well?" Jesus could read this man like a book. He had been there so long he had almost forgotten why! Instead of waking every morning with an eagerness and expectancy for healing and health, he had become sour. His reason for living was to try and find enough energy to stay close to the pool and watch others get healed.

Whenever there was a moving of the water, it was "every man for himself," and this man was always left behind in the dust. He watched resentfully, envious of those who had friends and family to help them, bitterly aware that he had to do it alone.

His way of handling his pain was to see himself as a victim of a selfish family. He perceived them as neglecting their responsibility to help him into the pool. In fact, he felt he was a victim of everyone who had mobility. Thirty-eight years and still a cripple...he blamed the whole world!

His answer to Jesus' question betrayed him. He should have answered a simple "Yes!" But to a person with the mentality of a victim, life is never that simple. Instead, this man took the opportunity to complain...to blame everyone for his condition. This way of handling life was so deeply ingrained in him, that even when Jesus healed him and he was called in by the religious authorities for questioning, he blamed Jesus for making him walk on the Sabbath day (John 5:11). One would think that his joy at being healed would have spilled over and confounded the questioners. Instead, he presented himself as a victim of the miracle worker, who got him into trouble with the religious authorities by healing him.

This man perceived life as happening *to* him; he saw himself as being thrown about like a football from one situation to the next. He did not accept any responsibility for or lay claim to any choices as his own. His perception of life was that other people were responsible for the way things were in his life. It was others who made him sad or, sometimes, happy. He saw himself as always the helpless victim, an object to be pitied by all who would listen to his story.

The Victim Mentality

Today, in the twentieth century, we live in a society that seeks to handle its pains, failures, and sins in exactly the same way as the man in the story. In living a life that is going nowhere, depressed and in despair, it is fashionable and easy for us to find someone else to blame. And so, we blame our parents for the way they raised us or we blame those who have abused us.

We lay the blame for our present misery at the feet of a mate who divorced us or a partner who cheated us in business. Society views the addict not as someone who is personally responsible for retreating from life's hurts into drugs and alcohol, but as the victim of his upbringing, of society itself, or even of disease. The murderer is often considered a victim of society who has experienced an attack of "temporary insanity."

Many people living with the mentality of a victim are so immersed in their denials of personal responsibility that they are blind to the truth of their condition. Like children, they solemnly shake their heads..."It's not my fault; she made me do it."

This is the mentality behind many disintegrating marriages. Any pastor would agree that he hears it in almost every counseling session. Invariably, each party blames the other for the condition of the marriage, which, of course, is precisely the reason things are the way they are.

"It's all my husband's fault," sobs the wife. "If only he would change...." The husband then comes in and uses his appointment to rail at his wife, taking her apart for the counselor. He is confident that if someone could make her see how badly she is fulfilling her role as a wife, then the marriage could be saved!

While pastoring in Brooklyn, I often listened to men who blamed their locality for their inability to make a success of life. They were convinced that if only the welfare people or some benefactor would move them out of their neighborhood into a new part of town, they would find overnight prosperity. They never saw themselves as responsible for the condition of their lives.

The victim mentality can often be heard in the lunchroom. A man who has been a grouch all morning complains loudly and graphically about how a truck cut him off on the way to work. Because of that, he has been angry and upset for hours. He is making it plain to his fellow workers that he is not responsible for his snarling and snapping; his bad mood is all the fault of an anonymous driver who briefly passed through his life!

We all have our little expressions that make another person seem responsible for our ill humor. We say, "She makes me sick!" or "He's a pain in the neck!" or "She makes me mad!" The simple fact is, no one makes us angry. *We are the ones totally responsible for our moods, words, and actions.*

Who Are the Real Victims?

There are those who all of society would agree have been truly victimized. These are the children now being abused by sadistic parents, who lash out at them out of the deep spiritual emptiness of their own hearts. Our audiences are filled with those who were abused as children...mentally, emotionally, physically, and/or sexually. They are like young saplings that were twisted and have grown over the years into bent trees. They wrestle with problems and ways of looking at life that began all those years ago.

Still others have known hurts that, like a knife, have cut deep into their souls...the wife whose best friend stole away her husband...the young couple whose life was plunged into a nightmare when a drunk driver killed their child...the woman who has been raped...the parents of the teenager who was killed by a drug addict for ten dollars...the business partner who was cheated out of his life savings and left as a pauper...the pastor who poured his life into building a church from a handful of folks to a congregation of thousands, only to see it split and scattered by a jealous associate.

For such people as these, we use the term, *victim*. It is a very old word, coming to us from Roman temples where the animal sacrificed on the altar was called the *victima*. When we say that a person is a victim, we mean that they have been sacrificed on the altar of someone's selfishness, greed, or wickedness—and in being sacrificed, something has died inside of them.

From Victim to Ruler

The Lord Jesus Christ brings hope and new life to such people. He comes to save us, not only to an eternal heaven, but to a totally new outlook on life in the here and now; He frees us from bondage to what others have done to us.

But, much more than that, He makes us reign in

7

our lives as kings: **...much more those who receive the abundance of grace and of the gift of righteousness will reign in life through the One, Jesus Christ** (Romans 5:17).

The word "reign" is a very strong word; in the Greek language it is "to reign as a king." It means to hold supreme power, to exercise sovereign authority, to prevail, and to dominate. Jesus comes to those who once were a bloody sacrifice on some altar of evil, and resurrects them at the very place of their wounding to ruling authority over their circumstances.

Such a person who has been resurrected from the altar of someone else's wickedness by the power of Jesus Christ will truly agree they have been *victimized*, that awful thing did truly happen to them. But they no longer see themselves as a *victim*, for they are no longer dead on the altar, but are seated with Christ in the place of authority in their life.

Tragically, there are many who are believers in the Lord Jesus and, yet, they live their entire lives with this mentality of a victim. They never come into the fullness of the abundant, overflowing life which Jesus came to give.

Where Do You Stand?

Are you paralyzed by choosing to handle life's problems with the mind-set of a victim? How have you handled the problems and hurts that have victimized you in the past? If you are not reigning in the strength of Christ Jesus, you will see certain attitudes in your outlook on life.

1. *Victims see the hurt which was inflicted on them in the past as the key to the meaning of their life today.* They explain their present life, their attitudes, and every failure, not in terms of their responsible choices, but in terms of what was done to them. They see themselves as the "victima," the helpless sacrifice, unable to live a normal life.

2. *It follows, as we have seen, that people with a victim mentality will not accept responsibility for their actions.* They blame other people, past or present, for their choices or assumed inability to choose. "After all he did to me, I can never be a complete person again!" "If you had been raised in the same home I was, you would be in the same state I am in today!" "If XYZ had not happened, life would be wonderful...but who could know happiness after that? Life has been a living hell ever since."

3. *You will find that the victim mentality operates out of an unresolved anger root.* You have never forgiven whoever hurt you, and the anger you have carried has been suppressed into deep resentment...now expressed quite irrationally at everyone and everything in general. Often, this suppressed anger produces a life blanketed by depression.

4. *This anger can also show itself in a belligerent attitude:* "I have a right to what I want; after what I have been through, life owes me. They didn't care if they hurt me, and now I don't care who gets hurt." This is often the philosophy behind the choices which lead to addictive behavior or to cheating on a spouse. It is the same thinking that justifies cheating on taxes—it says, "Let the other man pay; the country owes me."

I have heard this rationalization from the man who steals from his employer. For him, it isn't stealing. He sees himself as a victim of grave injustice, so his victim mind-set computes that his employer owes him!

5. *The victim, in an effort to ward off a repeat performance of the hurt, is generally suspicious of everyone, building impenetrable walls to make sure no one will ever get close enough to cause the pain again.*

6. *People with a victim's mind-set are filled with resentment.* Self-pity, with its paralyzing fantasy of what might have been, actually releases poison into their physical bodies. They become tired, drained of energy, and listless.

Today, Jesus comes to us with the same question He asked the crippled man at Bethesda: "Are you in earnest about being made whole? Do you really want to be totally alive?" And, like the man at the pool, we often sullenly respond, avoiding all reference to our own responsibility in the matter..."It's XYZ's fault that I am in this wretched state. After what they did to me, what else could you expect? They hurt me and have ruined my life for the last twenty years."

Grasp the Healing Hand of Jesus

The hope in this story is that, even though the man at the pool had given up, mentally paralyzed as he saw himself sacrificed by other people's selfish neglect, Jesus still healed him! However set in concrete his mind was, he could still respond to the voice of Jesus. Wherever you are in life, the living Jesus can reach you and make you whole. He can bring you out of the crippling mentality of being a casualty of another person's actions.

With His Word, Jesus called the man by the pool at Bethesda out of a life paralyzed by the mentality of a victim. The man grasped hold of that Word and was made whole. Jesus will do the same for you today.

Chapter Two

FREEDOM FROM GUILT

There are others who have become victims of their own past failures. Some have been through a divorce and have given up all hope of finding a "real" life again. Others may have seen their lives crumble through bankruptcy, and now they cannot move on to a new beginning. These people have confused failing with being a failure, and they now live in the twilight world of "If only..." and "What if...."

Perhaps it was falling into sin and public exposure which caused some to retreat into shame...shame of the sins that are ever before them, keeping them in the cringing pose of condemnation before God...shame that paralyzes and forbids them to face life with God's forgiveness.

Perhaps it is the abortion that no one knew of that still haunts your nightmares these many years later. It could be the lie which was never discovered...the degree gained by cheating that went undetected...the affair which was never uncovered, but still hangs like lead on your conscience. These secret sins feel like a nail in your shoe, crippling your walk through life. Many nights you lie awake in the silence and hate yourself. You live with thoughts of "If only I hadn't...," and you limp through life a victim of what you did.

Then there are those sins which are public knowledge: The prison record that brands the man for the rest of his life; the adultery that was dissected by the whole community and fueled discussion at the prayer meetings for months after the event; the man who embezzled from his firm and, even though the money has been paid back, lives in loneliness and shame, skulking in the shadows lest someone should recognize him.

Perhaps you are the victim of your own stupidity and the cruelty of self-righteous vultures. Is there life after a public sin?

Miracles of Mercy

In these last years, what we have missed in the proclamation of the Good News is the incredible generosity of God's love toward us. He pardons every sin and does not bring them to His remembrance.

Our problem is that we nestle into our victim mentality and refuse to take responsibility for receiving God's pardon. Yes, you did sin. Now, take full responsibility for your actions and choose to accept the full pardon that God gives through Jesus Christ. If you have any doubt as to whether God could forgive such a great sin as yours, remember Jesus forgave even those who crucified Him.

It amazes many people when they realize that the great men of God in the past sinned and found themselves in the trash can of life. God not only recorded their sin in the Scripture, but He also recorded His compassionate redemption of their lives—so that we might have hope in our despair.

Abraham, when approaching the border post of Egypt, and knowing that the Pharaoh was always looking for beautiful women for his harem, turned to his wife and disowned her! He told the border guards that she was his sister, and he left her to be taken by the Pharaoh into his stable of women.

His story was partly true, for he had married his half-sister, but in telling a portion of the truth, he lied, and also left Sarah to the horrors of an eastern harem. Surely he must stand as the greatest cad, liar, and disloyal husband of the Bible...yet God made him the Father of Faith!

This Bible account is not just a nice ten-minute gem to be shared at the Wednesday night Bible study, but instead, is the word of hope to our hearts as we look on the shameful things we have done in our past.

Moses, in his zeal to stand up for the right, became a murderer sought by the FBI of his day. He ran for forty years, until God arrested him and gave him the commission to bring Israel out of Egypt! His story is not a fairy tale, but a sober fact of history.

David, the king of God's choice, brought Israel from being an obscure group of loose-knit tribes-people to being the greatest nation of the Middle East...by infusing them with faith in God. Then, when more than fifty years old, with his fighting men warring at the front, David's passion became aroused for the woman next door. She was Bathsheba, the wife of Uriah, his dearest friend and most loyal soldier.

David and Uriah had been fast friends since they were both in their twenties and, more than once, Uriah had been ready to lay down his life for David. Yet, with Uriah fighting his battles on the front line, David began a lustful affair with his wife.

When Bathsheba became pregnant, David attempted to set up the appearance that Uriah was the child's father, but all chances to accomplish this failed. So David sent his best friend back to the front lines with a sealed letter to Joab, the commander-in-chief, containing orders for Uriah's own death. Joab complied with the order from his king and placed Uriah in a position where he was outnumbered in battle and killed.

David was an adulterer and a murderer. Yet, when he asked for God's forgiveness, he received it, and he stands today recorded in the genealogy of Jesus Christ. God's epitaph reads that David was a man after God's own heart!—not because he committed adultery, but because David knew God loved him in spite of his sin, and he dared to repent and receive God's love and forgiveness.

Peter, the chief of apostles, was one of the three best friends that the true Man, Jesus, had on earth. However, when Jesus needed that friendship more than at any other time, Peter loudly proclaimed that he did not know Him, punctuating his statement with curses and oaths. When it came to being a friend, Peter's actions said to Jesus: "It is not to my advantage to know You now. You are an embarrassment to me and I will have to leave You to Your fate." Yet, Jesus freely forgave and restored Peter, and six weeks later he was the first preacher of the Church.

Each of these people was a candidate for obscurity. Naturally speaking, they would spend the rest of their lives cowering before God and avoiding the eyes of men. But the energy of God's love and grace was greater than the worst that they could do. And we must face the painful fact that each of these people was a believer...a believer who sinned in the light of all that they knew of God!

Beyond Forgiveness

You cannot be a victim of your past sins except by your choice. God's grace is greater than the worst you have done. He waits for you to choose to receive His forgiveness. And it goes beyond forgiveness, for God takes the worst we have done and uses it for good, if we will let Him.

For example, I used to be an avid organic gardener. In our kitchen, we had two garbage pails—mine was the smelly one! I collected all the leftovers from the table, all of the inedible vegetable leaves, even the fish that was not eaten, and I worked them into my compost heap. Within a year, the refuse and embarrassment of my kitchen had become the richest soil in the garden.

God has a compost heap where He takes all our sins and failures and redeems them! It was out of Abraham's fear that he came to really know faith. Out of Moses' great failure came an understanding of the mercy and love of God that was thousands of years ahead of his time. David wrote many of his greatest psalms after he had called on God for pardon, and it was only after Peter's fall that he was able to know himself and to depend on God's grace and power.

There is a sense in which God only uses failures. It is not that He glorifies sin, but rather, He uses our fall to cause us to discover a weakness. This weakness then becomes a receptacle of His strength in a way that could never have been before our crash.

Chapter Three

JOSEPH,

A VICTORIOUS VICTIM

The Bible is full of case histories of God's dealings with men and women like ourselves, who had been deeply hurt or abused in life. One young man was Joseph, who could easily have perceived himself as a victim. Instead, he came to know the power of God by forgiving his abusers and rising above his pain.

In choosing to continually surrender himself to God in every painful situation, Joseph not only became the ruler over his circumstances, but the ruler over Egypt. From this position, he blessed the entire world! His story is found in Genesis 37-50.

Dysfunctional Beginnings

Joseph was raised in loneliness; he endured rejection by his brothers throughout his boyhood and as a teenager. When he was seventeen, his brothers sold him to slave traders. But he came to the point of embracing his circumstances and rising above victimization and rejection to become the second-in-command of Egypt. He found the ability to forgive his brothers and overcome self-pity, so much so that he was a blessing to the whole world.

He grew up in a family that was fractured and confused—four families trying to live together as one, with walls of jealousy between them. His father, Jacob, was polygamous, having four wives. Rachel, the only wife he really wanted, could not bear him any children, while the other three wives produced one child after another!

Finally, in her old age, Rachel gave birth to Joseph. Because he was his father's pride and joy, Joseph was immediately the object of his brothers' hatred. He occupied the position in the family that each of them had vied for. And, even if they had been kindly disposed towards him, the age gap was enormous—some of them were old enough to have been his father.

His father did not help the situation, continually doting on him, gifting him with the coat of the firstborn, marking him for tribal leadership. If this were not enough, add to it Joseph's mystical dreams, indicating the family would one day bow before him...dreams he shared at the breakfast table!

Joseph's mother died giving birth to another son, which left him all the more alone. And his father, in his own grief for the only woman he had ever loved, was, to all intents, absent.

The Deciding Factor

During those years of boyhood, Joseph learned from his father and, later, from his grandfather, Isaac, of the revelation of God that had been given to Abraham, his great-grandfather. It was the revelation of God's unconditional love toward man, a love which could not be earned or deserved, but came to man at God's initiative and was as unchangeable as God.

As Joseph listened to the words of his father and grandfather, his faith in the God of unconditional love matured. *With all the hellish things that ripped and tore at his life, the fact that he was loved of God and the object of His care enabled Joseph to look beyond his circumstances and rest in the God who actively worked on his behalf.*

Being taken into Egypt in chains to be sold at auction in a slave market could have made him a bitter man, who would spend the rest of his life seeking, in fantasy, the hurt of those who had hurt him. He could have had the mentality of a victim.

If he had seen himself as a victim, he would have defined the rest of his life in terms of the hurt inflicted by his brothers. He would have seen himself as not responsible for anything that happened to him from the time of the kidnapping.

If Joseph had had this destructive outlook on life, it would have shown itself when his owner's wife made herself sexually available. Day after day, she tried to seduce him. The victim mentality, resentful of Potiphar, his owner, would have seen himself as deserving her. His action would have said to Potiphar, "You haven't suffered like I have. How would you like to be someone's slave in a foreign land? After what my family did to me, I deserve some pleasure in life—and I am taking it wherever I can find it."

A person who believes he is a victim of life's circumstances sits pouting in self-pity, childishly asking why things had to be as they were. He rides the endless merry-go-round of "If only things were different," while fantasizing about the one who victimized him. He sees them hurting as much as he has hurt—and more.

We know this is not the way Joseph thought. If he had seen himself as a victim, we would never have heard of him. He would have died an unknown, bitter slave in an Egyptian jail.

Facing the Facts and Forgiving

When it is our own family who has abused us, or our brothers and sisters in Christ, we sometimes find it difficult and painful to admit that we were abused by them. So deeply do we believe that these are the ones who should have been there to protect and support us, we deny to ourselves that it ever happened. This leads to all manner of spiritual, mental, and emotional problems.

Joseph squarely faced the awful, terrifying truth that, out of malice, his own brothers had sold him into slavery. Years later he simply and bluntly told them, "You meant it for evil...."

The first act of authority we exercise as rulers working with God in the hurts of our lives is to forgive those who have been active in hurting us. For some people, this will mean reaching back into childhood to forgive the abusers and molesters of their early years. For others, it will mean forgiving those who have hurt them in their adult lives.

Somewhere in time, very soon after his brothers sold him into slavery, Joseph forgave them for what they had done. He defined his understanding of forgiveness at the end of the Genesis story, when he was second-in-command to the King of Egypt. His brothers came to him, terrified that he would execute them now that their father had died.

Joseph's response was, **Am I God...?** (Genesis 50:19, The Living Bible). He saw clearly that their judgment was not in his hands, but in God's, who said, **Vengeance is Mine, I will repay...** (Deuteronomy 32:35; Romans 12:19). Forgiveness is releasing the one who has hurt us into the hands of God, relinquishing our assumed right to carry out vengeance.

Recently, in one of my meetings, a young woman in her twenties came to me with a notebook that had four pages filled with names, each with a line through it. She said that after I had spoken on forgiveness the previous evening, she had written down every person who had hurt and abused her, knowingly or unknowingly, during her childhood and as a teenager, and had solemnly released each one to God. It had taken most of the night, but she stood before me radiant with a joy that she assured me she had never known before.

Forgiveness is not saying the abuser was right; it is simply submitting to God's unconditional love and recognizing that He is at work in the life of our abuser, as well as in our life. It is releasing our offender into His hands for Him to work in them as He will.

Joseph understood that his brothers were responsible to God for what they had done, and he was now responsible for what he did with them and with the abuse they had handed out to him. All of us are responsible to forgive—that is, to release our offenders to God for Him to work in their lives as He wills.

As soon as we have taken the injustice done against us and placed it into the hands of the Judge of all, we can turn and move forward in life. We no longer waste time and spiritual energy resenting the abuse or fruitlessly wishing it to go away. *We are ready to be workers together with God.*

God is not hindered by wicked men, but only by our self-pity and resentment, and our giving in to evil as we refuse to work with Him in bringing about His plans of love and good.

Chapter Four

CONFRONTING GOD

We cannot be free from the crippling shackles of the victim mentality until we have the answer to another question. Reading this story of Joseph, we find ourselves asking, "If God loved Joseph and is all powerful, why did He allow this to happen? Why did He not stop the brothers and make everything right?"

Some of you who are reading this have wondered why God allowed you to be beaten and abused...why He allowed your mother to be absent in a drunken stupor most of the time.

Others are looking at their own wrong choices in life and asking why God allowed them to make those choices. A young woman asked me, "Why did God allow me to marry Joe?" She sobbed as she told how her husband beat her until she could hardly walk. "If I knew there were some meaning to what is going on, then maybe I could accept it and get on with life," she said.

We must look beyond the surface of our questions and face the truth of our feelings. We are not only asking Him "Why?" We are also asking, but not daring to voice, "How could You do this to me? You have all power. How could You let this happen to Your child?"

In these questions there is a terrified helplessness. A divorcee looked at me in horror, "If God is behind all of this, then I don't stand a chance! I am not only the victim of what my ex-husband did to me, but I am the victim of Almighty God Himself!"

A Public Relations Nightmare

Historically, the Church has not helped us here, for we have been taught that this is indeed the way things are. We have been told that every cruel and vicious evil to rake across our lives is God's strange strategy of love. The Church has taught the world to label every tragedy caused by nature on a rampage as "an act of God," while telling those inside the Church that the terrible tragedy is "the will of God."

South Texas is often subject to devastating flash floods which have taken lives, destroyed homes, and left hundreds of families without possessions or

helter. A local newscast showed a tragic moment
n the life of one family as their teenage son was
pulled from the tangled bushes where the swollen,
aging current had finally dumped his lifeless body.
Adding to the horror of the moment, the camera
panned to the drowned man's sister, who was being
estrained by her family from running to his body.
We heard her agonizing sobbing and the hoarse
cream, "Give me back my brother!"

The next scene was of an older woman who had
ost all her possessions in the flood and now stood
n the mud of what once had been her home. She
was sadly saying, "...But what can a person do? It is
he Lord who sends every tornado and flood, and
he best we can hope for is to pick up the pieces and
go on till He sends the next one."

I shuddered at her words...words the reporter left
without comment as a religious commentary on the
ragedy of a lost son and a destroyed home. The
iewer was left to believe that the Christian revelation
of God was of One Who delighted, with the sweep of
His hand, to take loved ones and life's possessions
rom us. It was a damning slander against the God
Who is revealed to us in the Lord Jesus Christ. It
gnored the Jesus who stood against a storm that
hreatened to take lives and rebuked it, bringing it to
ilence and stillness. Yet, this slander is wholly
believed by many who call themselves Christians.

If we believe the slander, then inevitably we will sit paralyzed, blaming Satan and everyone else for what is wrong in the world...but especially blaming God. If, indeed, it is God who has offered us as victims on His altar, what is there to do but shrug our shoulders in fatalistic despair, waiting for whatever may happen next, and inwardly cursing Him for what He has already dumped on us.

If our God and Father is the One who brings the tragedies into our lives, killing our children and destroying our homes, then He must be labeled as the infinite Child Abuser...as the model for all earthly abusers and violators to follow.

Did God plan the evil that has befallen you? Do Christians worship a God who sits in His high heaven scheming with infinite wisdom to hurt, abuse, violate, and crush them to despair? Did He give strength to the father, who sexually abused his innocent child? Did He empower the rapist who violated the housewife? Did He put the idea in the head of your business partner to cheat you out of your life's savings?

Did He weave the circumstances which caused your child to be killed by the drunken teenager? Or worse, is He a weak and helpless deity, shrugging in impotence as He turns His head away from our tragedies lest He should see and be embarrassed.

If this is the God Christians worship, then certainly it is neither safe nor wise to give ourselves to Him. Life then becomes a hopeless attempt to escape the clutches of this infinite sadist, this divine monster! Our only other alternative is to become as sick as He and join the company of the religious masochists who are taught to welcome His thrashing.

Truth...or Consequences

Instead of slandering God by placing the cries of this world's anguish at His door, we must take the sin of man seriously. The first revelation of Biblical Christianity is to show us what is wrong with the human race. It tells us that mankind fell, that man sinned, and he is now set against the love plans of the God who created him. By default, man is now fighting the blueprint of his architect—and he is pursuing a pathway of self-destruction.

The truth is that outside of the salvation that comes to us from God in Jesus Christ, we will all destroy ourselves and our neighbors. The tornados, hurricanes, volcanos, floods, and earthquakes are merely a physical expression of the spiritual state of man, who is the lord of the planet.

God did not originate the evil that has come into your life, nor did He empower those responsible for doing it. You and I live in a fallen world, a world of people making imperfect and selfish choices. Some

33

people have and are, right now, planning evil against us in order to make selfish gain or to attempt to give their own empty lives some kind of sick meaning. We live in a self-centered, greedy society, which corporately and privately is making faulty choices.

We must come to terms with the reality that life in a sinful world is not fair. The hurt that has come into your life is, at best, the fallout of a bent society disobeying God; at worst, evil men, out of the evil of their hearts, deliberately did it to hurt you.

I remember one man who looked at me with agony in his eyes. He asked, "But why didn't God stop the evil from coming into my life? Why didn't He stop me from making such stupid decisions...decisions which I have been paying for ever since? He's Almighty, isn't He?" And a young woman who had been raped sobbed, "Why didn't He strike my violators dead?"

God made mankind in His image and likeness, and the awesome reality of our free will is at the heart of what that means. We are not programmed like the rest of the creation. To take away that free will would be the end of the human race; we would then be robots, God's puppets. What we want is for God to take away some other people's free wills— and we can be sure there are people who are praying He will take away ours!

Why does God allow the tragedies of life? There is no answer to that question, *because it is the wrong question*. Man is responsible for his wickedness, not God.

Chapter Five

DIVINE COOPERATION

Does God then stand helpless before the evil designs of wicked men? No! The miracle is that He actively works His love agenda within the evil choices of men and, *as we place our trust in Him,* He achieves His end in our lives. Joseph triumphantly said to his wicked brothers at the end of all his troubles, **You meant evil against me, but God meant it for good...**(Genesis 50:20).

The first ray of hope that enters my trashed ambitions and dreams, after the troubles and tragedies of life have swept through, is the understanding revealed by the Holy Spirit that God sits at the council table of man and works in and with his free choices. This incredible God is there when we exercise our free will and when our enemy makes his free choices against us.

God is there in the decisionmaking of the heart, when we freely make our foolish and selfish choices. He is there when those who are wicked in their intent are planning their evil deeds, and, to their utter confusion, He uses their evil for good. As the God of all love, His active energy of love is limitlessly seeking to turn every free choice we make, as well as every free choice made against us, to our highest good and His glory.

Faith That Reigns

Simple, childlike faith does not look only *at* what is happening, but *through* it to see God invisibly at work, taking the evil men have planned and turning it for good. Faith reaches through the evil, the hurts, and the senseless tragedies of life, and accepts what God is doing with them and in them.

Now, when I say that God is with us, we must not think of Him as a nurse patting our head and saying, "There, there..."! He does comfort me, but not by sympathizing with me in my frustration and hurt; nor does He join me and wring His hands along with mine saying, "If only that had not happened," or "If only you had listened to what I was saying!"

God is active and aggressive in His love, a warrior God. *When we will freely surrender to Him in the situation of pain and hurt in which we find ourselves, He will leap into it and make it His.* He takes over the

situation that is the source of our grief and sorrow—
a situation caused by the sinful choices and plans of
men—and announces that it is now His situation!

In this place of pain and hurt He will bring to
pass all His wise plans of love for us. God declares
war on evil on the very stage that evil has set up: He
gate-crashes the evil strategy and turns it to His ends
of joy and peace.

There are many things we cannot change...our
parents, our childhood, a divorce, the death of a
loved one, the selfish choices of other people, or
wrong decisions we have made. Looking at the
results of our own choices and the hurts that others
have inflicted on us, we do not become paralyzed
victims, nor do we blame God.

Instead, we ask Him, "What is Your love doing
with this mess?" He didn't originate it, but He is in it
with us to bring about His love plans. God is not
against us in this; He is with us, seeking to bring about
a greater good than we could ever imagine...a good
that will frustrate all the designs of evil against us.

The victim mentality accepts what was done to
us as the final word on the matter and sits paralyzed
and helpless. The faith that reigns in life, on the
other hand, chooses to surrender the present situation to God, transforming the trial into God's stage,
where He has chosen to work. *Faith refuses to*

concede victimization as the final statement of our life, but only as a weigh station en route to the goal of His love plans.

Faith faces the reality of the darkness and does not spend any time fantasizing about what might have been or what will be...not even what God may be doing. Rather, in faith, we choose to be workers together with God in this present moment—whatever it now holds.

The victim passively resigns to hopelessness in the face of the triumph of evil. But our submission to God is the beginning of real activity, and must never be thought of as a passivity that simply accepts what is happening as the inevitable will of God.

Overcoming faith is not a stoic gritting of teeth to go through it, praising God, while inwardly resenting every moment! It is the faith that looks back and sees that He was with us, working out His plan of love in every hurt of life that evil persons inflicted on us or our own sin and foolishness brought upon us. And it is actively accepting what God is doing in the situation in which we now find ourselves, while not resigning ourselves to it.

Reigning in life is offering ourselves to God in the midst of any situation, and in that way, to cooperate with what He is doing and to be co-workers with Him. It is intelligently cooperating with His love, wisdom, and power, which we dare to believe are now working in the circumstances we face.

God's Word is Your Final Destination

Even as Joseph was being carried into slavery, he believed the dreams of his teenage years were the Word of God to him. He knew that neither the pit, slavery, nor prison, were the final destination his God of covenant love had planned for him. But he did not fantasize about a future that as yet was not. Rather, Joseph embraced the present, just as it was, on his way to the future, and became a co-worker with God in the present moment.

In my book, *Spiritual Burnout*, I describe this adventure of divine cooperation in a parable:

Imagine the Christian life as taking place on the side of a mountain. There are various camps of believers all over the slopes, each group discussing the biggest problem to anyone who lives on the mountain: at regular intervals, rocks of all shapes and sizes roll down on the camps.

The discussion which dominates all of the camp meetings is, "Where do the rocks come from, who is rolling them down on us, and what do we do with them?"

Some believers look at the approaching rocks and whimper with fear. They are very unhappy and want the rocks to change course, evaporate—anything—so long as they go away. At the prayer meeting, these frightened believers beg everyone to pray for them, because the evil rock-throwers are attacking again. "Pray that the rocks will go away," they beg.

These believers have an expectancy of God that is not based on truth and, therefore, will never be realized. Their concept of the Gospel is that Jesus will remove all the rocks that roll down the mountain; their definition of peace is the absence of rocks from the horizon.

Another group of believers looks at the rocks and sighs, "This is our cross to bear, we will accept it patiently!" Their testimony to the other people on the mountain is that their God loves them so much that, on a regular basis, He throws rocks at them. They are the fatalists disguised as holy persons. Their whole philosophy is that what is to be will be.

These believers have no joy and very little happiness. It is difficult to get excited about a God Who throws rocks at His children! They live in a state of spiritual exhaustion and confusion, struggling to survive in a world of falling rocks and, at the same time, believe that God loves them.

Still another camp of believers, although closer to the truth, are also heading for disaster due to the way they handle life. They mock the fatalist, crying, "You must be crazy to think that God throws rocks at people He loves! We don't believe God wants these rocks to fall on us. In fact, we believe that our faith can make the rocks disappear and never return again!"

The way they understand faith is that it is a power God has given them to make the mountain exactly the way *they* want it...and they want happiness, with no rocks in sight! An extremist in their group might see a rock coming and say to his neighbor, "There is no rock there. Do not even mention rocks around me, or my faith will be destroyed." When the rock rolls over him, he refuses to budge in his confession; and when people ask if the rock hurt him, he denies that a rock came anywhere near him.

If he is not so extreme, he would approach the rock a little differently. He, too, would say that God did not throw the rock—it was the evil rock-throwers that threw the rock. However, also believing that faith is a power for his personal use, he would attempt to use his faith to dissolve the rock. He rebukes it and declares it a non-rock! When the rock rolls over him, he is shaken.

Seeing his failure to dissolve the rock, other members of his church will say that he did not have enough faith, and that is why the rock rolled over him. He then feels that God is as embarrassed over his poor performance as his fellow believers are, and he wonders if God has rejected him for his lack of faith.

Wanting his fellow believers to accept him and to continue in his reputation as a man of faith, he might hide the fact that a rock has just hit him. By doing this, he begins the lonely road of mask-wearing, which is one of the first symptoms of living a spiritual lie.

There are congregations in every city of these types of believers. Some live life being crushed by the rocks that roll down the mountain, desperately clinging to the truth that God really does love them and gives them the strength to bear the trials and torment that He purposely sends their way. Others, though correct that God is not the rock-thrower, erroneously believe that they can manipulate God to do things their way.

What they have all missed is that the Gospel is, first of all, the announcement of covenant relation-ship—*we are called to know God personally.* Our faith, by which He works in our lives, arises out of that relationship. This real faith is ultimately destroyed by unscriptural, traditional ideas of men, or formulas that allegedly make God do as we say.

God is not responsible for the falling rocks, nor will He be manipulated by false confessions of faith. What He has for us is so much more! He desires us to know Him, and out of that intimacy with Him will flow all the covenant blessings He has promised in His Word.

The believer whose faith is born of this intimate, covenant relationship with the Father looks at the rock rolling down the mountain and initially feels uneasy. He might feel a twinge of fear and wish that the rock would go away...he doesn't like rocks! But he stops himself from following the thoughts of fear and the desire to run. He tells himself that there is more here than a falling rock. He chooses to see all the facts, which include more than the rock.

He knows that the God he has covenant relationship with is all-powerful, that He is greater than all of the rock-throwers or the rocks they hurl at him. He also knows that Jesus has risen from the dead and has overcome every enemy. In the light of these facts, his position is that the rock is another opportunity to show the glory of the Lord Jesus...to show one more time that all rock-throwers are defeated.

Faith never falls apart at the approach of the boulders of life. It is when rocks are rolling that faith shows up the best. With praise to God, Who is his all-knowing, all-present, and all-powerful partner, and to Jesus, the Conqueror of the rock-throwers, the believer with faith stands in the path of the rock and exercises his God-given authority over it as it comes. He makes the choice to be a ruler through Jesus Christ, rather than to be a victim of the rock.

With a shout of triumph, he asks, "What shall we do with this, Lord? How are You going to be glorified this time?" This man, in union with his God, is the master of the mountain God ordained him to be. The altar on which the evil rock-throwers intended to sacrifice him is destroyed, and God's plan of love reigns in his life.

Chapter Six

JOINING WITH GOD

Do you despise and wish revenge on those who abused you? Do you find the mentality of a victim filling you with resentment towards those around you, while you feed yourself with self-pity?

It is never too late to readjust your understanding of life. Are you ready to throw off the victim mind-set and begin to know the power of God enabling you to reign in life?

The word, "repentance," in the original language basically means "taking a second thought." It is realizing that the first thought was wrong and turning from it to accept a whole new view of things. If you find yourself in the last paragraph, then it is time to repent, to take a "second thought" about your life.

We begin by turning our faith to the God who loves us unconditionally. He is infinitely on our side and has demonstrated His love in dying for us. He is now committed to us in unbreakable covenant to achieve His love plans for us, in us, and through us.

This God Who loves you, Who has revealed Himself in the Lord Jesus and His covenant blood, is everywhere present in all places and all times. He was with you as you went through the horrors of your life, whatever age you were. He has loved you through all the tortuous paths you have traveled because of your own reactions to what happened to you.

We must then recognize that we are personally responsible for the way we have looked at our lives and the attitudes that have arisen from our percep-tions. We call resentment and self-pity, our envy of others, and our suppressed anger at God by their proper name, "sin." We receive His forgiveness, which is already given in Jesus' bloodshedding and resurrection; we deliberately lay all the sin aside and, in the strength of the Holy Spirit, we refuse thoughts that would continue to look at life in this way. And God forgives us, cleansing us from all sin.

It is time to do what the lady in my meeting did, to take a notebook and write the names of those who have hurt us. One by one we release them to God and pray that they will come to find His salvation, even as we have.

Next, we deliberately take a leap of faith, which looks through the immediate circumstances and chooses to believe that God is at work here and now, turning this situation into His arena of blessing. We make the choice to embrace what God is doing in the situation, knowing that

1. Evil men made choices in their selfishness and we have been hurt;

2. God then chooses the arena of their wicked choices to achieve His good; and

3. We make a deliberate faith choice to turn from our self-pity and be a worker together with Him in this situation.

Triumphantly, this person who is walking out of the victim's prison says, "Here I am, with all that has happened, all I did, she did, he did, and what everyone else has thrown into the pot. This is the position I find myself in. God, I choose now to accept this situation, exactly as it is, as the stage on which You are going to produce your work, and to frustrate and silence evil."

Having made that choice, the next time your self-pity begins to rise, you point back to the moment when faith chose with God that this would be the platform on which He works.

It is time to see that, through it all, He was and is with you, loving you with all-powerful love. Take another look at your life and see how, in spite of all that was done to you, in spite of all you have done to yourself, He has led you to Himself and to His love. *Accept your acceptance by Him.*

Ask the Holy Spirit to open your mind so that you can grasp and understand that God has loved you with limitless and unconditional love through every moment of your life, and He now calls you to receive it. Let the Holy Spirit open your eyes so that you see Him in the hours and days of trauma, as you did not and could not have seen Him when you were going through them.

It is time to offer yourself to Him, to actively embrace life now. You must boldly face the rock and see what God wants to do through you. You become God's co-worker, cooperating with Him Who loves you...Who is working in you and in your circumstances to bring to pass His love agenda.

To do this will bring relief—and the beginning of a process of healing that will continue over the next weeks and months. Set aside time every day in which you realize His love for you; realize and welcome the Holy Spirit within you, causing the love of God to increase and abound and be applied directly to the wounds of life.

From the depth of self-pity, depression, and despair, you can walk out of the prison in which you have lived these many years. As a free person, you can begin blessing your world in the unique fashion for which you have been molded all of your life.

This is the faith that looks back and sees that He was with us even before we knew Him, working out His plan of love in every hurt of life...those that evil persons inflicted on us and those which our own sin and foolishness brought upon us.

It is time to deal, once and for all, with the sinful attitudes that have plagued our lives and crippled us. Just as He stood before the man at the pool of Bethesda, the Lord Jesus stands before us now and asks us if we really want to have a new life. Respond to His Word! Rise from the altar where you were sacrificed, and take up the victim's bed of self-pity! Begin to walk in the resurrection life of the Lord Jesus, victimized, but *no longer a victim.*